DARING
AVALANCHE
RESCUES

AMY WAESCHLE

Consultant:
Dr Tim Durkin
Mountain Rescue Medical Director

Raintree is an imprint of Capstone Global Library Limited, a company incorporated in England and Wales having its registered office at 264 Banbury Road, Oxford, OX2 7DY – Registered company number: 6695582

www.raintree.co.uk
myorders@raintree.co.uk

Edited by Lauren Dupuis-Perez
Designed by Sara Radka
Production by Katy LaVigne
Printed and bound in India

ISBN 978 1 4747 5392 0
22 21 20 19 18
10 9 8 7 6 5 4 3 2 1

British Library Cataloguing in Publication Data
A full catalogue record for this book is available from the British Library

Quote Sources
p.10, "Colorado skier felt life fading during 3 hours buried in avalanche." *Denver Post*, 30 March 2013; p.14, "Avalanche survivor on rescue effort: 'It was a miracle.'" CBS, 29 January 2017; p.18, "Woman Buried Alive in Avalanche Saved by Quick Thinking, and Her Left Hand." ABC, 20 December 2012; p.22, "An Avalanche Survival Story." James Mort, 5 March 2015; p.25, "Snowmobiler buried by avalanche survives." *Seattle Times*, 4 March 2007; p.27, "Snow Fall: The Avalanche at Tunnel Creek." *New York Times*, 26 December 2012.

Acknowledgements
Getty Images: Ben Girardi, 24, Creativaimage, Cover, 9, Dennis Welsh, 21, Geir Pettersen, 20, Kennan Harvey, 19, Paul Burns, 11, Philipp Guelland, 28, Sathish Jothikumar, 26; iStockphoto: Cylonphoto, top 6, 23, fbxx, bottom 15, Figure8Photos, Cover, 18, frontpoint, top 15, lopurice, bottom 7, Lysogor, 4, top 7, back cover, nicolamargaret, middle 7, wakr10, Cover, bottom 6, yuelan, 25, ZargonDesign, 29; Newscom: DanitaDelimont.com, 8, 17, DFF, 12, 13, 14, Penny Kendall, 16, ZUMAPRESS.com, 22; Wikimedia: LarsEvers, 10

Graphic elements by Capstone Press and Book Buddy Media.

Rescues after avalanches

In most avalanche accidents, people
are the cause of the sliding snow.

Thunder rumbles, but there's no storm in sight. In fact, the sky is blue and the air is crisp and cold. So where is the sound coming from? A **slab** of snow has broken loose from the side of a mountain and is tumbling down. It is an avalanche!

Every year, avalanches kill more than 150 people around the world. Most victims are skiers, snowboarders and mountain climbers. They go into the wilderness to enjoy untouched snow. These areas can be quiet and peaceful. However, they can also be dangerous.

Most avalanches happen after a snowstorm or when the air warms up. These events can make the snow unstable. Areas where wind has pushed snow are especially dangerous. People usually cause avalanches. A skier, snowboarder or climber moves over an area of snow that is not stable. This causes a separation of the snow from the mountain. The slab of snow begins to slide on the broken surface. As it moves, it picks up more snow – and more speed. Within seconds, the snow is moving as fast as a freight train. It is powerful enough to uproot trees. When a person gets caught in an avalanche, it can be deadly.

slab broad, flat, thick piece of something; slabs of snow break apart to begin some avalanches

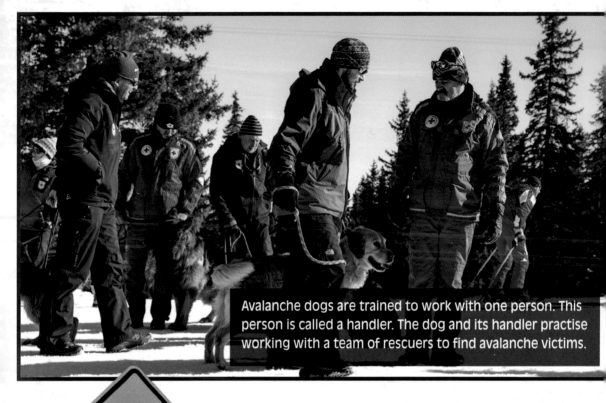

Avalanche dogs are trained to work with one person. This person is called a handler. The dog and its handler practise working with a team of rescuers to find avalanche victims.

AVALANCHE AREA

NO STOPPING OR STANDING NEXT 2 MILES

Being carried away by an avalanche is terrifying. Snow chunks become like boulders. The snow batters everything caught in its path. When the snow stops, it freezes like concrete. A person trapped inside cannot move. No one above the snow can hear the person shout. The only way the trapped person can survive is to be rescued.

But who will come to a trapped victim's aid? Avalanches often happen in remote mountain areas. There are often no roads. Rescuers sometimes come from far away. They may need to climb steep slopes. And they must hurry, because a person buried under the snow cannot survive for very long. Each rescue is different, yet each requires bravery, determination and skill. Uncover the minute-by-minute details of daring avalanche rescues from around the world.

Types of avalanches

There are three types of avalanches. Each type occurs in a different way.

Slab: A slab avalanche involves the entire top layer of snow. The top layer breaks free because the layer beneath it is weak and collapses. Slab avalanches are the most deadly. They can reach speeds of up to 130 kilometres (80 miles) per hour.

Slough: A slough avalanche usually happens after new snow has fallen. A small amount of the top layer of snow slides down the mountain. Slough avalanches are less likely to be dangerous than slab avalanches.

Wet: A wet avalanche often happens in spring when the snow melts. It can also happen after rain. The wet snow becomes heavy and weak. It breaks away and slides down the slope. Wet avalanches move slowly. People rarely trigger these avalanches.

CHAPTER 1

Buried alive in Colorado

Wilderness skiers hike up slopes using grippy rubber skins that attach to the bottom of their skis. The reward for their work is open slopes and untouched snow.

Skiers can access uncrowded slopes outside of marked ski areas.

Alex White and his friend Joe Philpott woke to a blue sky and fresh snow on 2 March 2013. They went up to Paradise **Bowl** at Cameron Pass, a mountainous wilderness area in northern Colorado. White skied down the bowl first. At the bottom, he turned to watch Philpott come down. Philpott started his **run** with a jump. When he landed, the snow cracked.

White saw a cloud of snow racing down the mountain. He tried to move out of the way, but the snow around him was too deep. He had enough time to put on his Avalung, a backpack with a breathing tube for use under the snow. Then the avalanche swept him up.

White tried to swim inside the sliding snow, but it was too powerful. He was carried more than 100 metres (328 feet) down the slope. When the avalanche stopped, he was completely trapped.

bowl valley or area of land that is low and that has higher land around it

run rider's turn on the course

State park rangers Andrew Maddox and Sam McCloskey were working at a snowmobile event nearby when they got a distress call from the local sheriff's office. The rangers took off on their snowmobiles. On the way, they got stuck several times. Finally, they reached the top of the avalanche. As they were searching for victims, a report came in from another group of skiers. They had found Philpott, but he had not survived.

Maddox and McCloskey feared that they would not find White alive, either. It had been more than three hours since the avalanche. It was getting dark. The sheriff wanted them to turn back. But finally, Maddox and McCloskey got a signal from an emergency device. They followed it to a pair of gray boots sticking out of the snow. They began to dig furiously. They heard a noise. It was White! The Avalung had worked. He was alive!

The team loaded White on a snowmobile and took him to safety. White's body temperature was dangerously low, but he survived. One month later, Maddox said he still got goosebumps when he thought about how close they came to missing White that day.

"The last thing I remember thinking was that I was going to die there, honestly."

ALEX WHITE

The Avalung is a device worn close to the body. If victims are buried by an avalanche, they can use the Avalung's breathing tube for air. This gives them more survival time under the snow.

Avalanche rescuers must work as a team to find buried victims. They access the site by snowmobile, helicopter or on foot and use radios and mobile phones to communicate with one another.

Avalanche at Hotel Rigopiano

When rescuers first arrived at the Hotel Rigopiano, they had trouble locating the building. The massive avalanche had wiped it off its foundations, and then crushed it.

The avalanche at the Hotel Rigopiano was so violent that it picked up parked cars and carried them down the mountain.

Guests at the Hotel Rigopiano in Italy were worried. On 18 January 2017, earthquakes had shaken the hotel. They had also caused avalanches. Guests wanted to go home, but **debris** blocked the roads. Then at 5.00 p.m., a huge avalanche crashed into the hotel, smashing it into pieces.

Giorgia Galassi and Vincenzo Forti were drinking tea in the hotel when the avalanche hit. Snow burst into the building. It shoved them into an air pocket. They were stuck deep beneath the ruined hotel and a layer of hard snow. Galassi and Forti were lucky. They were alive. But they were trapped without water and food.

debris scattered pieces of something that has been broken or destroyed

Aftershocks rumbled and heavy snow fell while thousands of rescue workers searched for victims at the Hotel Rigopiano.

In the middle of the night, an emergency team arrived. They had skied and hiked on snowshoes through a snowstorm. Paolo Di Quinzio led the team. When he arrived, all he found was snow. Finally, his team found some of the hotel debris. They started digging.

In the morning, more rescuers arrived. They dug tunnels and used listening equipment. They used trained dogs to sniff for the buried people. After 41 hours, there were no signs of life. But the rescuers refused to give up. Finally, after two days, they heard voices. It was Galassi and Forti. They were in an air pocket made by tree branches, ice and hotel debris. To get them out, rescuers had to dig carefully so the pocket didn't collapse. Ten hours later, rescuers pulled them from the ruins. Rescuers were also able to save 11 other people.

"We never lost hope that someone would come for us."

VINCENZO FORTI

Avalanche safety gear

After an avalanche, help is often a long distance away. For this reason, wilderness travelers carry three items that are essential if they are caught in an avalanche.

Transceiver or beacon: This small device can send out and receive a signal. At the start of the trip, each person's beacon is in "send" mode. If a member of the group gets swept up in an avalanche, the others in the group switch their beacons to "receive". The rescuers then follow the signal to the buried person.

Probe: This is a folding pole. It is made of lightweight metal. After the beacon finds the area where the person is buried, the probe is poked into the snow. When the probe touches something, searchers know where to dig.

Snow shovel: Even if a person is buried under only a small amount of snow, the packed snow is hard to move. A sturdy snow shovel can turn an hour of digging by hand into mere minutes. This time difference can save a life.

CHAPTER 3

Avalanche dog to the rescue

One avalanche rescue dog's powerful nose can sniff an entire 1-hectare (2.5-acre) snowfield in 30 minutes. It would take a team of 20 humans 4 hours to cover the same area.

With 11 chairlifts, Crystal Mountain Resort is the largest ski resort in Washington, USA.

Emily Anderson and two friends went skiing at Crystal Mountain Resort in the state of Washington, USA, on 17 December 2012. More than 1 m (3 feet) of new snow had fallen in 30 hours. Anderson and her friends were excited about the fresh snow.

They started to ski down a slope when Anderson heard a crack and a pop. The snow around them began to break loose. Anderson realized that she was in an avalanche. The sliding snow pushed her into a tree. Then she was under the snow. Luckily, before the snow stopped moving, she could move her hand. She scraped some of the snow away from her face. This made an air pocket. She could breathe. She screamed for help, but no one could hear her.

Avalanche rescue dogs can sniff out a person buried 9 m (30 feet) deep.

Anderson had not been skiing **off-piste**. She was not wearing avalanche safety gear. Her ski partners also had no rescue gear. They had been buried by the avalanche too, but only partly. They dug themselves out and quickly called for help.

Within 5 minutes, the ski patrol arrived. They brought Newman, an avalanche rescue dog. Newman found Anderson's scent right away. The ski patrol team used their probes to pinpoint Anderson's location and dug her out. Luckily, she was not hurt.

"Avalanche dogs are the best way to find somebody like Emily. This woman is lucky.**"**

PAUL BAUGHER
CRYSTAL MOUNTAIN
SKI PATROL DIRECTOR

off-piste land around or near a ski area that is not checked by a ski patrol

Avalanche rescue dogs

All dogs have a powerful sense of smell. But avalanche rescue dogs must also have other special traits. "Avy dogs" must be able to work without stopping for several hours. They must learn to ride on a chairlift and a snowmobile. Avy dogs must love to work and be ready to go, even in the middle of the night. Most avy dogs are golden retrievers, Alsatians or border collies.

Avy dogs need to practise their skills. Ski patrol members play games of hide-and-seek. To do this, a ski patrol member will sneak away. Then he or she will dig a hole deep in the snow and hide inside it. Then, the avy dog is set free and told to "find". The avy dog sniffs until it finds the person's scent. It starts to dig. Its tail wags faster. There's a person inside! The avy dog is rewarded with lots of praise. Sometimes it will even get a treat.

Avalanche rescue dogs must learn how to ride chairlifts.

CHAPTER 4

Nowhere to go in Switzerland

Ski resorts maintain their slopes to prevent avalanches. Off-piste areas are not maintained. This makes them much more dangerous.

James Mort was skiing in Switzerland on 30 January 2015. A storm had dumped almost 1 m (3 feet) of snow over two days. The avalanche danger was high. Mort and three friends spotted a run through some trees. There were no ski tracks there. Mort wanted to be first and "get fresh tracks".

To get to the area, they would have to **traverse** an off-piste area. This was dangerous, but the group decided to go. They had skied the area before in the same conditions and felt it was safe.

During the traverse, Mort heard a muffled "whump" sound. This is the sound of snow collapsing. It can signal a layer of unstable snow. The group stopped and talked, but decided to keep going. Mort skied the run first. The **powder** was so deep that he could barely see. When the land dropped into a steeper section, Mort caught some air. When he landed, the top layer of snow broke away.

Skiers and snowboarders who hunt for fresh powder are called "powder hounds".

traverse travel across

powder snow that is very light and dry

Avalanche forecasters

Before heading into an avalanche-prone area, travellers listen to the avalanche report. This tells them if the snow is stable. There are five levels of danger: low, moderate, considerable, high and very high. Avalanche forecasters are the people who set these levels.

An avalanche forecaster must understand **meteorology** and mountain **terrain**. Many forecasters have also worked on a ski patrol. Many of them have university degrees in meteorology or engineering. To make a forecast, avalanche forecasters travel into the mountains. They dig a pit in the snow, looking for weak layers. If a lot of fresh snow falls over a weak layer and the slope is steep enough, avalanches are more likely.

Avalanche forecasters have an important job. Skiers, snowboarders and others rely on them. Forecasters try to let people know where and when avalanches are most likely to happen. But they can never make exact predictions, and avalanches are always a threat.

meteorology science of weather

terrain surface of the land

At first, Mort tried to out-ski the avalanche. But the snow caught up and ploughed over him. Mort reached up with his ski pole. Then the snow set up like concrete. One of Mort's friends called the ski patrol and they started to search. They spotted the tip of his ski pole. They were able to dig down to his face so he could breathe. Two patrollers arrived, and together they dug Mort all the way out. Even with five people digging, it took almost an hour.

❝'Okay,' I thought to myself, 'You're dead.'❞

JAMES MORT

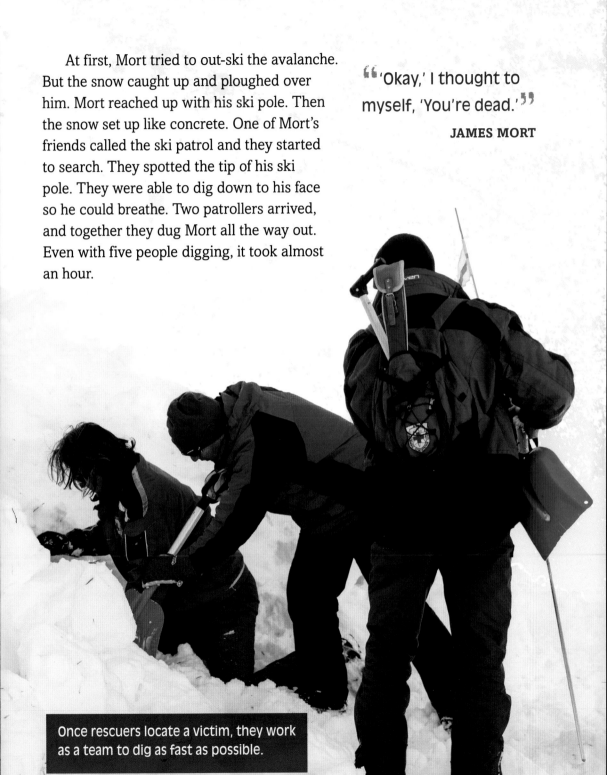

Once rescuers locate a victim, they work as a team to dig as fast as possible.

CHAPTER 5
Surviving an eight-hour burial

Some snowmobile riders like to play a game called "high marking". Each rider in the group tries to ride higher on the slope than the previous rider. This activity can cause an avalanche.

Ryan Roberts was on a snowmobile trip through Flathead National Forest in Montana, USA, on 4 March 2007. Roberts, his uncle and a friend were exploring the Jewel Basin area. All of a sudden, a slab of snow broke loose. Roberts tried to outrun the avalanche on his snowmobile before jumping off. He tumbled downhill along with the snow. When the avalanche stopped, he was buried face up under 1.2 m (4 feet) of snow.

Roberts's uncle and friend quickly began a **grid search**. They were wearing beacons, but Roberts was not. After two hours, they began to lose hope of finding him alive.

Roberts's uncle called the sheriff, who sent a team to help. He also called family members to help search. Finally, after eight hours, Roberts's cousin hit something solid with his probe. The rescuers began to dig. They found Roberts. Amazingly, he was still alive, but he was suffering from **hypothermia**. The rescuers warmed him by a fire. Then they rode him out on his uncle's snowmobile to a waiting ambulance.

> "I guess I was just allowed to live another day."
>
> **RYAN ROBERTS**

How to survive an avalanche

No matter how much a person plans ahead, he or she could still get caught in an avalanche. Even experienced skiers can get caught in a slide. Most people are trapped in an avalanche when conditions are "considerable", since many people don't hit the slopes when the risk is "high" or "very high". Most victims can stay alive for 15 minutes under the snow. After that, there is no more air. Here are three things people can do to stay alive if they are caught in an avalanche:

1. Try to either get off the slab of sliding snow or grab a tree. If those two things fail, swim hard. Try to stay near the surface.
2. As the slide slows down, try to make a pocket of breathing space. This will give you a few minutes of air.
3. Push a hand upwards. This hand may break through the snow, signalling rescuers.

grid search organized search method that uses probes to locate buried victims

hypothermia life-threatening condition that occurs when a person's body temperature falls several degrees below normal

CHAPTER 6

Eager for powder

More than 9 m (30 feet) of snow falls on the Cowboy Mountain area each year. The snow usually stays until late spring. This makes it a popular place for winter sports.

Elyse Saugstad, a professional skier, was invited to ski Cowboy Mountain in Washington, USA. She was excited. A storm had dumped 53 centimetres (21 inches) of new snow. The avalanche forecast was "considerable", but the sky was blue and the wind was calm. On 19 February 2012, Saugstad went with a group of local skiers into the wilderness.

Saugstad skied second, stopping at a halfway spot. When the third person was skiing down, a gigantic **crown** of snow broke loose. Saugstad was carried away in seconds. She pulled the cord on her **airbag** backpack. She tumbled around and around as the avalanche continued down hundreds of metres.

> "I had no ability to control what was happening to me. I was being tossed over and over and over."
>
> **ELYSE SAUGSTAD**

crown highest part of a slope

airbag bag that is filled with air; airbags can be used as cushions or safety devices

Ski patroller Chris Brixley received the call that skiers had been caught in an avalanche. He sent out four ski patrollers and two avalanche dog handlers.

The remaining skiers in the group turned their beacons to "receive". They followed the path of the massive slide. But there was no sign of their friends. Finally, at the **toe**, their beacons started to beep.

Before heading out on a ski trip, skiers should make sure their avalanche beacons are working properly.

toe where an avalanche stops

The airbags in Saugstad's backpack had kept her close to the surface. Rescuers followed her beacon's signal and dug her out. She was alive. The three other group members caught in the slide died. Saugstad said the airbag saved her life.

Avalanches are rare, but when they happen, they can be deadly. When a person gets buried by an avalanche, they may only have minutes to survive. Their lives may depend on the determination of their rescuers.

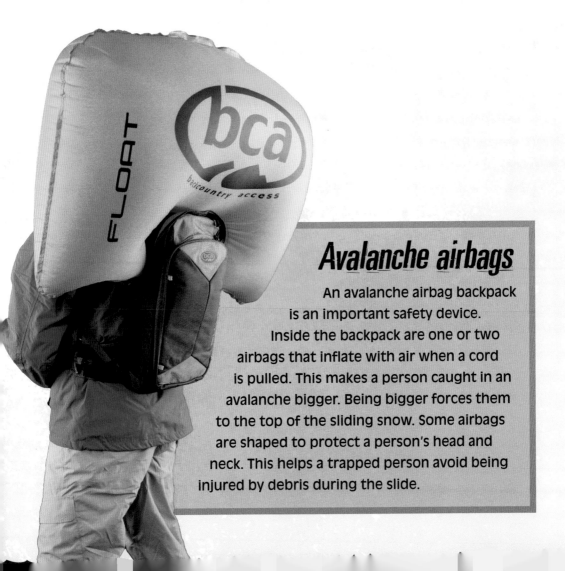

Avalanche airbags

An avalanche airbag backpack is an important safety device. Inside the backpack are one or two airbags that inflate with air when a cord is pulled. This makes a person caught in an avalanche bigger. Being bigger forces them to the top of the sliding snow. Some airbags are shaped to protect a person's head and neck. This helps a trapped person avoid being injured by debris during the slide.

Glossary

airbag bag that is filled with air; airbags can be used as cushions or safety devices

bowl valley or area of land that is low and that has higher land around it

crown highest part of a slope

debris scattered pieces of something that has been broken or destroyed

grid search organized search method that uses probes to locate buried victims

hypothermia life-threatening condition that occurs when a person's body temperature falls several degrees below normal

meteorology science of weather

off-piste land around or near a ski area that is not checked by a ski patrol

powder snow that is very light and dry

run rider's turn on the course

slab broad, flat, thick piece of something; slabs of snow break apart to begin some avalanches

terrain surface of the land

toe where an avalanche stops

traverse travel across

Find out more

Books

Crushed!: Explore forces and use science to survive (Science Adventures), Richard and Louise Spilsbury (Franklin Watts, 2013)

Mountains (Geographics). Izzi Howell (Franklin Watts, 2017)

Snow and Blizzards (Weatherwise), Robyn Hardyman (Wayland, 2014)

The Worst Avalanches of All Time (Epic Disasters), Suzanne Garbe (Capstone, 2012)

Websites

**http://www.nationalgeographic.com/environment/
natural-disasters/avalanches/**
Read more avalanche facts and information.

http://beaware.sais.gov.uk
Learn how to stay safe in the snow and mountains.

http://easyscienceforkids.com/all-about-avalanche/
Learn more about the science behind avalanches.

**https://www.mountaineering.scot/safety-and-skills/
weather-and-avalanche-forecasts**
View current weather and avalanche forecasts for mountain areas in the UK.

Index